Emotional Eating

How to Stop Overeating, Dieting, and Binge Eating Naturally!

Dennis E. Bradford, Ph.D.

Emotional Eating

Publisher's Notes

ISBN 978-1-940487-03-8

Contents

Books by the Same Author

The Concept of Existence
The Fundamental Ideas
Mastery in 7 Steps
How to Survive College Emotionally
A Dark Time
Personal Transformation
The Three Things the Rest of Us Should
      Know about Zen Training
The Meditative Approach to Philosophy
How to Eat Less – Easily!
Compulsive Overeating Help
How to Stop Emotional Eating
How to Become Happily Published
Belly Fat Blast with Anna Wright
Getting Things Done
Weight Lifting
Love and Respect
12 Publicity Mistakes that Keep Marketers
      Poor
It's Not Just About the Money!
40 Top Marketing Mistakes

1: Introduction

If you were obtaining more satisfaction from life, temptations to indulge in comfort eating would *automatically* be reduced. In this book you'll learn how to enjoy life more. If you apply its recommendations, they will quickly result in less, or no, emotional eating.

This is not a book about food. If you are an emotional eater, your chief problem is not about what you eat. Your chief problem is that you do not yet skillfully handle negative emotions.

The purpose of this book is to encourage you to (i) improve your understanding of emotions and (ii) use that improved understanding to do better emotionally.

Doing well emotionally, flourishing emotionally, is the result of using a set of skills. If you are not yet flourishing emotionally, that's only because either you have not yet learned how to flourish emotionally or you have not yet done what you understand you should do. This book will enable you to understand what is required and how to do it. That will not only automatically undermine emotional eating, but also it will greatly increase how much you enjoy life. *There's nothing wrong with you. All that is required is learning what to do and using what you have learned.*

It's good to be skeptical, but it's bad to be negative. Permit me a brief explanation of each.

With respect to skepticism, please question everything in this book and test it for yourself. Since what you are about to learn really works, you'll lose your initial skepticism. Since you may have been insufficiently skeptical in the past, you may have unintentionally picked up beliefs about emotions and emotional well-being that are false. It would be a good idea simply to set aside all such ideas and approach the ideas presented here with a more open mind. If you find the ideas presented here unpersuasive, you can always go back to your old ideas; on the other hand, if you find them persuasive, you can replace your old ideas with better ones. Isn't that reasonable?

With respect to negativity, drop it whenever you notice it. Why? It's nothing but a self-interested tactic used by the ego/I to make itself more powerful. Since all ego/I's are dysfunctional, it's a toxin that never works. Since to increase the power of the ego/I is to increase separation and since separation is always the cause of dissatisfaction, be assured that the more negative someone is, the more dissatisfied that person is.

Learning should be fun as well as result in beneficial consequences. I hope that you enjoy this book and really benefit from its lessons.

2: Self-Image

Stopping emotional eating requires letting go of your self-image. I don't mean altering it. I mean dropping it.

Surprised? Shocked?

The only way we are able to improve our understanding is by clashing alien ideas against those familiar ones we are so attached to. Unless you are willing to do that, this book will be useless to you. However, if you are willing to do that, this book may enable you to improve your understanding and help you apply that improved understanding to how you live so that the quality of your life improves.

Either outcome will be a win for you. If your familiar ideas withstand the test, then you may have more confidence in them. If they fail the test, then you may junk them in favor of more fruitful ideas.

This book, however, is less about theory than about practice. Still, there must be some theory because nobody who is rational will adopt a new practice without understanding how it may be of benefit. So please decide to open up to what may be some initially unusual ideas.

If you don't, you'll just stay stuck to your old ideas and nothing will improve. If you don't improve what you are doing, you'll keep getting the same old results; if you don't improve what you are thinking, you'll never improve what you are doing.

Have you been told for years that the way to make improvements in the quality of your life is to improve the way that you think about yourself? Once you begin to accept the idea, for example, that you really are a nonsmoker, quitting smoking becomes easier.

That is the usual way that self-improvement is supposed to work. I'm not denying it: it is possible to make some improvements in your life by improving what you believe about yourself, which is your self-image. Once you have improved your self-image, you will tend to behave in accordance with that improved self-image.

That method, however, usually results in only minor, temporary improvements. It's rational to want only to make the smallest adjustments possible to attain what you desire. The reality, though, is that merely tinkering with your self image cannot yield emotional wisdom.

It's a bit like tinkering with your eating habits by using a reducing diet.

Suppose that you want to reduce your percentage of body fat and go on a reducing diet. The odds that you will have a significantly lower percentage of body fat five years from now are 50 to 1 against you. Furthermore, even if you wind up in the winning 2%, you'll have had five years of struggle.

If you have ever tried dieting, that may explain why it almost certainly failed to work for you. The lesson: *never* go on a reducing diet.

In fact, it's even counter-productive. Here's why: suppose you go on a reducing diet and lose 20 pounds. Unless you are simultaneously doing intense exercise of the right kind, those 20 pounds will be about 10 pounds of muscle and 10 pounds of fat. When you eventually go off the diet, you'll not only regain those 20 pounds, but most of those regained pounds will be fat instead of muscle. Therefore, even though you'll wind up at the same body weight, you'll have a higher percentage of body fat than you did when you began the diet – and that's the opposite of the result you wanted.

However, you may be thinking that we are all different. That's true. A method of losing a significant percentage of body fat and sustaining that loss for over five years that works well for me may not work well for you.

I do not claim that the method in this book is the only method that ever works for anyone. I do claim that, for nearly everyone, it offers the best chance of reducing or stopping emotional eating permanently.

The reason for my confidence is that the method attacks what causes the problem of emotional eating. Instead of tinkering with minor adjustments at the edges of the problem, it goes straight to the heart of the problem. If you eliminate what is causing condition X, you'll eliminate X. That makes sense, doesn't it?

If you are at least middle-aged, you probably have already discovered for yourself that superficial or minor changes don't result in beneficial results that last. For example, have you ever lost at least 20 pounds and kept them off for five years? Have you ever bench pressed 300 pounds? Have you ever increased your net worth to over one million dollars? If so, very good.

Then what happened?

You enjoyed your new quality of life – no doubt about that.

But then what happened? You adjusted to your improved life and that was it. Nothing essential changed.

The temporal world, the world of "Becoming," is in ceaseless flux. Nothing abides.

Therefore, even if you had the power arrange everything exactly as you wanted it, that successful arrangement would soon fall apart. Success never lasts.

Despite its popularity, success is the wrong model for genuine happiness. [I argue for this thesis in my Mastery in 7 Steps.] I'm certainly not against success. It's just that it cannot work for genuine happiness (authentic happiness, living well) – as many people have discovered for themselves after years and even decades of hard toil. Sages have been telling us this for at least 2500 years.

The chief reason why you are interested in emotional eating is because you want to break your bondage to it, to free yourself from it. The reason you want to free yourself from it is because you are dissatisfied with the way your life is now. Excellent! What better motivation is there for doing better than dissatisfaction?

The obstacle of bondage to emotional eating is a disguised

opportunity to increase your level of genuine happiness. In other words, if you take this opportunity to free yourself from bondage to emotional slavery, you'll not only enjoy a decreasing percentage of body fat, but also you'll have learned a critically valuable lesson about how to improve the overall quality of your life significantly.

Why not re-frame this issue? If you keep asking, "Why do I suffer from emotional distress that stimulates overeating?" your brain will supply answers to which you'll likely attach. If, instead, you were to keep asking, "How can I do better emotionally and reduce or eliminate emotional distress?" your brain will also supply answers, which means that there's no reason to be stuck with a poor understanding of emotions. Why not be kinder to yourself than that?

Improving emotionally is not selfish, either. Why? If you master what it takes to improve the overall quality of your life, you'll *automatically* become a better role model for others, particularly loved ones who observe you frequently. By directly helping yourself, you'll indirectly be helping them.

It's not easy to help others. Telling others what to do is often ineffective and sometimes counter-productive. Instead, it's usually much more effective simply to show them what to do. So, if there are others you love, why not use that as additional motivation to free yourself from emotional bondage?

No emotional bondage, no emotional overeating.

Your self-image is all about egocentricity. By definition, it's all about you. Loving others isn't at all about you: it's about giving to others what is best for them without expecting or hoping that you yourself will gain anything in return. Love is about giving; love is not about taking. [For a lot more about this, see my Love and Respect.]

By learning how to detach from egocentricity, you'll not only be able to break free from the bondage of emotional eating, but you'll automatically become better at loving others.

Detaching from egocentricity is about breaking bondage to compulsive thoughts (conceptualizations, judgments, propositions, statements, beliefs, evaluations, and so on). **Although letting go of compulsive thoughts is simple as well as beneficial, it is difficult to do.** However, the more that you master doing it, the more free you'll become from emotional eating and other emotional poisons and the more loving you'll become. The purpose of this book is to help you do that.

As literate, civilized humans we are all attached to our thoughts about ourselves. There's no question about that. [I have argued for this elsewhere, including in <u>Mastery in 7 Steps</u>.]

Let's use 'sages' to denote those people who live freely and peacefully, who are not slaves to compulsive thoughts.

What sages do that the rest of us fail to do is to liberate themselves from bondage to compulsive thoughts. They shift from being thought-centered to being awareness-centered. Instead of being fixated on judgments, they go beyond judgments. Instead of incessantly conceptualizing, they often enjoy freedom from conceptualization ("no-thought"). There's no agreed-upon terminology here, but I hope to make clear in what follows what this really means.

This doesn't mean that they cannot think when thinking is necessary. It means that they are free from *having* to think incessantly, they are free to think or not to think. The rest of us are slaves to thoughts.

What's this got to do with stopping emotional eating?

As I explain in what follows, **there is an egocentric thought at the heart of every emotion. Therefore, there is an egocentric thought at the heart of every negative emotion. Since negative emotions are the cause of emotional eating, dropping that egocentric thought stops emotional eating by dissolving what causes it.** So learning how to let go of egocentric thoughts includes learning how to let go of negative emotions that are necessary causes of emotional eating.

Isn't that an exciting possibility? By understanding how to release yourself from the grip of negative emotions, you will become able to free yourself from all their bad consequences, of which emotional overeating is just one.

Those of us who are still bound to compulsive thoughts drag those thoughts into all our experiences. That is a very heavy burden. Instead of continually enjoying fresh experiences, we incessantly subsume experiences under concepts or labels, which deadens them. Life becomes wearisome, boring, tiresome, dull and flat.

This is the opposite of all the talk about the lightness of Being.

Let's agree to use the word 'form' to refer to whatever we are able to single out for our attention. Whenever we are able to answer the question 'Which one am I thinking about?' the answer will be a form. It may be a thought ("I like strawberries") or a perceptual object ("that is an oak tree") or a dream object (such as the green blog from last night's dream that was trying to ingest me) or a remembered object (mother's face) or an imagined object (what the house will look like when it is built) or, possibly, even an abstract object (such as the number 4 [not the numeral '4']). Every object is a form.

The critical mistaken assumption that we all initially make is that we shall become happier by attaching ourselves to certain forms while avoiding certain other forms. So daily life becomes a process of trying to obtain what we like and to avoid what we don't like. What this means is that we unintentionally become slaves to our egocentric desires. Since it's better to be free than a slave, we remain dissatisfied regardless of our temporary successes. It's unnecessarily sad that most people simply grow old and die without realizing the alternative.

What's the alternative? It's the way that sages live. They open Becoming to Being so that their lives are centered in "silence" rather than "noise." **Words, concepts, and thoughts are noisy forms of Becoming, whereas silence is the language of Being.** Another way to put this is to say that sages transcend the temporal (Becoming) by opening it to the eternal (Being, what is timeless).

It doesn't follow that forms are unreal and should somehow disappear. It's that sages experience forms from the domain of Being rather than from the domain of Becoming. Unlike the rest of us, they are not trapped in Becoming.

All forms are temporary, often fleeting. If you want lasting satisfaction, what sense does it make to attach to impermanent forms?

In one sense, freedom from Becoming changes nothing. Forms are still forms. It's not as if they are somehow replaced by something else or all disappear into a brown soup. In another sense, it changes everything. Before liberation from Becoming, forms were taken to be the whole of reality. After liberation, the whole of reality is taken to include Being as well as Becoming. Life forever becomes fresher, newer, lighter, and brighter.

So any given form will be taken as more than just another isolated form. Each form has an essence of Being; **each form is not isolated but an aspect of Being**. [I discuss this more in Getting Things Done; its appendix is devoted to the Being/Becoming terminology.]

That includes you. You are a form, too. Insofar as you feel isolated, you are lonely and suffer. (A good way to pass the time is to eat, so this feeling itself can fuel emotional eating.) You understand yourself as essentially incomplete or lacking, which is what spawns egocentric desires. You want to fill up the hollowness.

We all have a tendency to think, " I'd be happy if only I could have X" and, so, desire X. Even if you manage to obtain X, whatever it is, however, the satisfaction it provides won't last. You'll quickly adjust to having X and desire something else. Since whatever can be gained and also be lost, you'll also live in fear of losing X. This is a treadmill it's best to get off.

Sages, too, have preferences. The difference is that they are not attached to them. If they get something, they appreciate it. If they don't, it doesn't bother them.

It's the quality of experiences that changes rather than the experiences themselves. The thoughts sages have no longer necessarily contaminate their experiences.

How is all this related to your self-image? **Your self-image is nothing but a set of thoughts.**

You will still be able, if you want, to think the same thoughts about yourself that you had before, but you won't mistake them for the real you. The real you is neither a thought nor a set of thoughts. It is neither a form nor a set of forms. Since you are nothing less that Being, *the real you includes what is beyond Becoming.*

What is it? Although it can be directly or *non*conceptually apprehended, it cannot be thought or spoken. Why? To think is to conceptualize (sort, divide, segregate, classify, categorize). There's a logical difficulty with thinking, namely, it's impossible to think unity. Since thinking is inherently discursive or dualistic, unity cannot be thought. It isn't a form because it cannot be singled out. So nobody can tell you what Being is because language is conceptual.

When you realize that the real you includes more than a set of forms in Becoming, you will immediately stop identifying with a certain autobiography or life story or a certain body that supposedly persists for many years. That body had a beginning and will have an end. It exists in the domain of Becoming. You will fear the death of that form only if you continue to identify solely with it. If you fear being dead, that's only because you are not yet a sage.

Do you keep hoping for future fulfillment? If so, that's because of a less-than-satisfactory present. Most people are caught simultaneously fearing the future, since that's where death is, and hoping for the future, since that's where genuine satisfaction may be. Because stress occurs when forces pull in different directions, that's an unnecessarily stressful way to live.

Since all language comes from Becoming, it is impossible to use language to describe or conceive the transition from experiencing life from the perspective of being trapped in Becoming, which is where all conceptualizing occurs, to the perspective of experiencing life from Being. At best, words are nothing but signposts.

It's impossible to think yourself from Becoming to Being.

To realize Being directly, just stop the mind from discriminating. That is like waking up from a sleep and having all dreams vanish. I'm no sage and you shouldn't take my word for anything. In fact, you shouldn't take anyone else's word about Being. The point is to experience it directly (*non*conceptually, without conceptual filtering). When you do, the cause of emotional eating will instantly weaken. The more you live from Being, the less emotional dissatisfaction you'll experience. It is not necessary to experience *any* emotional dissatisfaction.

"Waking up" or "awakening" is simply all thoughts, which means letting go of attachment to thoughts. Since your present self-image is a set of thoughts, waking up includes dropping your attachment to it.

Your true Self is neither too fat nor not too fat. The real you includes what is beyond all forms, beyond Becoming. It's impossible to think (conceive), but it's possible to be aware of it. You are unimaginably more than you think you are.

Even if all this is so, what good is it? If it's impossible even to think Being, doesn't that just make freedom from emotional eating impossible?

No.   All it means is that it's impossible to think your way out of emotional bondage – and all that means is that it's impossible to think your way out of emotional eating. That's a dead-end.

If so, we have made a major gain in understanding in just this chapter. We have recognized an important dead-end. If these ideas are correct, we now understand what *not* to do. We've learned what doesn't work.

Let's ensure a positive attitude before considering what does work.

3: The Right Attitude

What's so important about a positive attitude? Even when we realize its importance and achieve it, why is it sometimes so difficult to sustain?

Contrary to what many people believe, we do not perceive what we perceive. **We perceive what we think.** In other words, we perceive only an interpretation of reality (what-is, what exists) rather than reality itself.

This explains why Being is the obstructed obvious. When we drop all thoughts, which obstruct Being, we are able to apprehend Being directly and instantly; it's obvious.

We are conscious of only a selection of what we sense; we experience only a fraction of what we sense. Our senses take in far more information than we attend to consciously. At least if we are to believe the scientists who investigate these matters, our consciously lived experience, our individual surreality, is, *at best*, only a selection from reality.

If so, it's easy to see how our attitudes might affect the selection, what we consciously attend to.

Please remember that our brains evolved for survival. If, in a given situation, your attitude is negative, if you feel threatened or fearful or angry, what you attend to in your surroundings will be different than if your attitude had been positive in those same surroundings. Examples of this abound in everyday life. **Experience feeds on itself.** Your brain is excellent at finding what you are looking for. If you are looking for danger, your brain will find signs of danger. If you are looking for goodwill, your brain will find signs of goodwill.

At least if you want positive experiences in your life, this is why having a positive attitude is important. Having a positive attitude fosters having positive experiences, which reinforce the positive attitude. It's a feedback loop.

Since positive experiences are preferable to negative ones, why is maintaining a positive attitude so difficult? Why isn't it automatic?

To understand the answer, ask yourself this question: "Do I usually think about what I am able to figure out?"

Of course not. Why would you think about something you have already figured out? What you usually think about is what you have *not* figured out, perhaps even what you cannot figure out. So, you are typically much more conscious of what you don't understand than what you do understand.

(Some researchers have speculated that our default condition, what we think about when we are not forced to think about other issues, is to think about interpersonal relationships. Because they are always difficult, they always provide fodder for the mind to chew.)

Though it's rewarding to have figured out solutions to our problems, it's no fun figuring out those solutions. Problem solving, consciously thinking, is hard work. We most enjoy our lives when we simply act without having to think about what we are doing. When we drop all thoughts and just do whatever we are doing, we enter "the zone" and directly experience a unified mind/body. Since suffering always requires separation and unification is lack of separation, there is no suffering in such unitive states.

So there's a kind of built in imbalance that explains our tendency to be negative, which is why most of us have to work at developing and sustaining a positive attitude.

When we are really enjoying life, we are not stuck trying to solve problems about breathing, finding shelter, providing food, finding a sex partner, combatting illness, dealing with aging, worrying about dying and death, and so on. When we are not enjoying life, it's solving important issues like those just mentioned that are exactly what we are thinking about.

Since issues like those confront us all regularly, we have to deal with them regularly whether we want to or not. It's having to deal with them regularly that threatens to erode maintaining a positive attitude. That's why, if you want one, it's important to *work regularly at creating a positive attitude.*

It's a commonplace that our lives occur only in the present moment. We cannot live yesterday now. We cannot live tomorrow now. Similarly, since we cannot be elsewhere now, our lives are right here rather than in some other place.

Notice that the **mind is never content right here, right now**. It is typically bored here in the present moment. It finds the here and now uninteresting. It constantly wants to flee to the future, to the past, or to dreamland.

If that's true, as you may determine for yourself by carefully witnessing the incessant rising and falling away of thoughts, are you already beginning to suspect that, when improperly used, the mind is an incessant source of discontent?

The more the mind remains undisciplined (untrained, unpurified, unrestrained), the more likely you are to feel dissatisfied in the present moment. Since the present moment is the only real moment, the more the mind remains undisciplined, the more you will feel dissatisfied. This explains why, although it doesn't have to be this way, **being dissatisfied is normal.**

When you are dissatisfied, why not enjoy eating something delicious as a distraction? After all, tasting and chewing some favorite food temporarily beats being dissatisfied, doesn't it?

Do you often find yourself rationalizing in that way? If so, it's easy to understand the direct connection between failing to train the mind and overeating.

4: Stress

Stress is natural. Whether physical or psychological, stress occurs when two forces in the same place are pulling in different directions.

It has always been a feature of human life. Since it, too, can directly connect to emotional eating, it's worth considering briefly.

The way to live well with respect to stress is to have neither too much nor too little. The **goal**, then, is to **manage stress properly**. By way of contrast, the goal is not to eliminate it, because the only way to eliminate it would be to die. It is no more intrinsically evil than it is intrinsically good. The middle way between too much stress and too little stress is the ideal.

Managing it properly means arranging our lives so that its consequences are beneficial rather than detrimental. Growing is a good consequence of stress, whereas becoming agitated is a bad consequence.

Stressors have changed from the Pleistocene to the Anthropocene [Cf. http://dennis-bradford.com/intellectual-well-being/the-anthropocene]. One of the key differences may be that, although we are not as frequently exposed to physical dangers as they were, we are exposed to more constant stressors than our ancestors.

Obstacles to relaxation (stimulants) are available twenty-four hours a day. For example, we are profoundly affected by sound. If you live in a city, you are constantly bombarded with the sounds of traffic, including sirens, and frequently music and construction noise. Radio, television, and the internet are available every minute of every day; if I'm not using them, my neighbor seems to be. Playing, squealing children often create irregular, disturbing noises. Stimulants raise blood pressure.

There are many other stimulants as well. Many people are addicted to the news, which is filled with stories that are deliberately chosen because they titillate or excite or disturb. We frequently stimulate ourselves with caffeine and its relatives as well as street drugs like cocaine and amphetamines. Who would want to go to a movie, a play, or a zoo that wouldn't stimulate us? Who would want to listen to a preacher, a comic, a teacher, or even a salesperson who wouldn't stimulate us?

Since few are immune to it, a frequently unnoticed stressor is time consciousness. The more we pay attention to watches and clocks instead of to whatever we are doing, the more stressed we are. There are enormous productivity advantages to be gained from timing performances, but they come at a cost and we humans have only been bearing that cost heavily since the development of clocks, in about the last two and one-half centuries.

The same goes for the other major stressors that cause worry such as separation from loved ones, aging, poverty, and ill health.

Thoughts generate a lot of anxiety, guilt, and stress. Our failure to control the mind causes stress-related illnesses of all kinds. The idea that mind and body are separate is a delusion.

How do you handle stress? What are your best methods?

There are a number of helpful practices.

One is to figure out ways how to sleep better. [For a discussion, see in chapter 7 of Belly Fat Blast.]

Another good way is to vacation well. The key to a good vacation is to vacate the mind, to empty it of thoughts. Why not give yourself a vacation every day? How? Use an effective body practice [such as the one discussed below in Chapter 8].

Exercise is a very productive way to alleviate stress. There are several different kinds of physical exercise that are helpful: fitness exercise, strength training, flexibility work, and moving meditations such as t'ai chi and other kinds of yoga. [I discuss these in multiple books as well as online in my blog and lasting-weight-loss.com.]

There are less common kinds of therapies such as hypnotherapy and biofeedback that may be helpful.

These kinds of practices are very beneficial. I encourage you to find ones that work well for you and make them habitual.

On the other hand, there are a number of practices that are unhelpful. Probably the most common is overeating. Eating a piece of pie or some cookies or ice cream is easy. Furthermore, the benefits are immediate.

Food is fuel. Using food as anything other than fuel is dangerous. If you routinely are too stressed and resort to comfort eating in an attempt to alleviate your stress, all you are doing, besides getting fatter, is temporarily alleviating a symptom. If you deal with the underlying problem, which I explain how to do in this book, you won't need comfort eating. There's nothing terribly wrong with an occasional serving of comfort food, but there's a lot wrong with a regular serving of it.

Similarly, drinking too much alcohol regularly is dangerous. ('Too much' means more than 2 drinks daily for a man or 1 drink daily for a woman.)

Similarly, using recreational, nonprescription drugs is dangerous, as is promiscuous sex.

Instead of relying on such external fixes, why not solve the stress management problem from the inside out?

The key to improved stress management is to assume responsibility by taking much greater and more effective control of both your external and internal environments.

Why not undermine the need for *any* comfort eating instead of heading for the refrigerator whenever you are bored, lonely, upset, or simply "down"?

I'm not suggesting that external practices aren't helpful. They can be very helpful. I've written about many of them elsewhere, including on the free resource lasting-weight-loss.com, which contains a lot of important, useful information about eating well, exercising well, and relaxing well.

In this book, however, I focus on what I have discovered is the best way to begin to take full control of your thoughts (rather than letting compulsive thoughts control you). It's not only simple, but it's easy to do.

Furthermore, I indicate alternative "body practices" as well that may be even more effective for you.

Once you start going down that path, your days of slavery to emotional overeating are numbered.

5: The Structure of Emotions

In order to understand why the kind of body practice I recommend in this book works to undermine emotional eating, it's necessary to understand the structure of emotions. [I also explain this in other writings, most recently in <u>How to Stop Emotional Eating</u>.]

Emotions are composed the three non-emotional parts.

Let's primarily focus on negative emotions. Negative emotions such as fear and anger can be useful. After all, if in some emergency situations, for example, you felt no fear when you should feel fear, you might fail to take life-saving actions. So, like positive emotions, negative emotions can have good consequences.

Nevertheless, since positive emotions do not cause overeating, negative emotions should be our primary focus in this book. They don't feel good; when we suffer from them, we want to get rid of them.

Scientists like Paul Ekman have studied facial expressions in different human cultures and have come up with 7 universal emotions among humans (namely, sadness, anger, surprise, fear, disgust, contempt, and happiness) of which only 1 is positive. (Note that using the word 'happiness' this way to refer to an emotion is at least somewhat peculiar.) Mother Nature seems to have equipped us to experience mostly negative emotions.

Emotions may be generated in multiple ways. An important one is that they are automatic evaluators that enable us to act quickly in emergencies. Whether emotions are stimulated by our apprehension of a situation that may be deleterious to our welfare (such as noticing an approaching forest fire or tiger), by remembering or talking about a past emotional event, by sharing an emotion empathically with someone else, or by deliberately assuming the physiological changes that appear with emotions until you actually stimulate the relevant emotion (as some actors do), or by some other way, there seems to be a kind of species wisdom embodied in emotions [Paul Ekman discusses this in Emotions Revealed, revised ed.].

Emotions are functional processes that come from our evolutionary or personal past that prime us to act quickly.

It certainly does *not* follow that emotions are always appropriate. Sometimes we feel one emotion when we should be feeling another. Sometimes we are feeling an appropriate emotion, but we are feeling it too strongly or too weakly.

Nor does it follow that emotions always result in right behavior; in other words, sometimes we act (show, display) emotions incorrectly. (Right behavior diminishes pain or suffering, whereas wrong behavior increases pain or suffering.) Sometimes we should override automatic evaluators with slower, reflective ones.

It's important to note that *emotions narrow our focus*. If someone socks you in the face and you fly into an intense rage, you'll instantly become less aware of your surroundings. Emotions block us from attending to all that we are sensing. They affect our surrealities.

Usually we don't challenge why we are feeling some particular emotion; instead, we seek validation for feeling that way by interpreting our environment in a way that validates that emotion. Although that can help keep us focused on some important problem at hand, it can also cause us to make poor decisions because we are cut off from a clearer, more neutral apprehension of our environment.

In theory at least, fully awakened sages never import past emotions into the present moment. It's not that they don't have emotions; instead, it's that they detach from them much, much more quickly than ordinary people. (I have witnessed this myself and it can be astonishing.)

If you have the kind of learning style that benefits from doing exercises, try this: for the next few days, keep a pen and paper with you and simply record your emotions. The record need not be anything elaborate, but record at least the emotion (assuming that you are able to identify it) and what triggered it. For example, "after her phone call on Thursday afternoon, I was sad to learn that her brother-in-law had died unexpectedly." This is a practical exercise in paying attention.

We've already covered enough territory to enable us to understand **the structure of emotions**.

First, what emotion would you feel if your beloved child had just been killed in an automobile accident and you didn't know about it?

It's a trick question. If you didn't know about your child's death, you wouldn't feel any emotion related to it. Your grief wouldn't kick in until you learned about it.

Once someone points it out, it's obvious that an emotion depends upon a judgment about the environment, some apprehension or other of whatever situation or state of affairs you take yourself to be in. You won't fear being killed by that tiger over there if you don't notice the tiger.

No judgment of the situation, no emotion. In other words, our emotions depend upon our understandings.

Second, suppose that it's snowing in Moscow right now. How do you feel about that? It's extremely likely that you have any feeling about it one way or the other. Of course, if you are stuck in a hotel in Moscow and have no chance of getting to the airport to make your flight, you may well be angry.

Once someone points it out, it's obvious that an emotion depends upon relating your understanding to yourself. **No egocentric relationship, no emotion.** In other words, the heart of every positive emotion is an egocentric evaluation of the form "*This is good for me*" and the heart of every negative emotion is an egocentric evaluation of the form "*This is bad for me.*" Emotions <u>never</u> occur without self-involvement. Your self (ego/I, ego) is your identification with form(s) such as a set of thoughts (your story or autobiography), emotions, or body.

If you are keeping a record of your emotions, notice how they always related some understanding of your situation to what you like or dislike. There are no exceptions.

If you think that there are exceptions, it's only because you are not recognizing the extent of the range of your self concept. In other words, you are failing to understand what you are identifying with. For example, you learn of yet more famine in Somalia and feel sad for the children there. You are including those children within your self concept; you are identifying with their impoverished condition. You feel bad because you think there are starving children in Somalia and you identify with their plight.

Third, emotions are experienced physically. Emotions have a bodily component. They involve physiological reactions. **Emotions are typically felt as**

physiological sensations in various parts of the body, often in the front of the body such as the throat or stomach, although you are probably familiar with what they can feel like in the back of the shoulders or neck or, even, as a pain in the ass..

This is what enables scientists to study emotions in other people by studying, for example, their facial expressions or linguistic reports of how they are feeling. More importantly, it's how we often understand the behavior of others. If I suddenly encounter you and you are grinning from ear to ear, I'll" read" you as being happy. If, on the other hand, you are stomping along with tense lips, narrowed eyes, and a ferocious scowl in your face, I'll "read" you as being angry.

Different people experience emotions in different bodily ways. Nobody else can tell you how, for example, you typically experience anger or sadness. *It's very important that you begin to become more sensitive to your emotional states.*

Please notice, for example, when you feel angry. Does your heart rate increase? Does your respiration increase? Are you able to feel your blood pressure rise? Do you feel your face redden? Are you clenching your jaw? Is your chin thrusting forward? Are you ready to move forward?

We talk about flashes of anger because emotional expressions are often quick or short, often just a second or two. They can be easy to miss in others as well as easy to miss in ourselves.

Again, even if emotions are universal among humans, there is no one single bodily state (such as a facial expression) that is reliable as an indicator what the emotion is (if any). Different individuals are, in fact, emotionally different. We may all experience the same emotions, but it's false that we experience them in the same way. Our behaviors and bodily states are different.

Since all emotions go with a corresponding mood, noticing your mood can help. If, for example, you are experiencing the emotion of sadness, your mood will be depressed.

It already may be obvious <u>how emotions can go wrong.</u>

First, we may misunderstand the situation. It's possible to think there is a tiger over there when there isn't – or to miss noticing it if it is there.

Second, what we take to be good or bad for us is relative. Something I think is bad for me may turn out good for me and vice-versa. Recall how many times this has happened to you. **The egocentric attachment is the heart of every emotion**. It's the referent of the 'for me' in either 'this is good for me' or 'this is bad for me.' One reason why emotions come and go is that our self-concepts are not as stable as we often think they are.

Third, the resulting physiological states can make living harder rather than easier. If I become fearful for no good reason and the hormonal cascade of the flight-or-fight response kicks it, it'll be a while before I'm back to neutral. Stress like that can become chronic.

Misunderstanding our own emotions, which seems to be more common among males in our culture rather than females, often leads to wrong behavior.

This is a sufficient understanding of emotions for understanding how to undermine emotional eating.

Let's examine three popular tactics that don't work well and then examine the kinds of tactics that do work well to undermine emotional eating and, more generally, to free ourselves from emotional bondage.

6: Three Ineffective Tactics

If emotions are not a problem, emotional eating cannot be a problem. So what should we do to ensure that, when they arise, emotions are not a problem?

The idea is <u>not</u> to try to prevent emotions from arising. Emotions are natural experiences; they are integral parts of our lives. If they had not contributed to our ability to survive, they wouldn't have evolved. So please let go of any thought of somehow eliminating, repressing, or suppressing emotions. Even if that were possible, it is not necessary and would likely be counter-productive.

What we are looking for is a method for maximizing the benefits of emotions while minimizing their costs.

When confronted with negative emotions or passions, first don't make them worse. It's like the saying about holes: "When you are in one, stop digging."

If you happen to be gripped by a powerful one right now, realize that it is temporarily making clear thinking much more difficult.

Here are 3 ways that it's possible to make them worse. Unfortunately, they are the common ways of dealing with unwanted emotions.

First, **avoid adopting a bad attitude.** What's a bad attitude?

It's one that attempts to avoid responsibility. The truth you must realize is this: "I am solely responsible for the quality of my emotional life." Nothing external to you, nothing outside you, can *ever* make you feel anything unless you decide to let it. Something happens (whether or not it's in your control), you notice it, and then you decide whether to react at all and, if so, how to react.

You may, in fact, put yourself through terrible emotional suffering for a long time without ever realizing that you are doing it to yourself.

We've come to understand that every emotion is composed of three parts: (1) a judgment about some situation or state of affairs, (ii) an egocentric evaluation of that situation, and (iii) a physiological sensation or set of bodily sensations. For example, (i) you learn that your mother has just been killed, (ii) you instantly think "this is bad for me," and (iii) you begin crying from sadness.

Even assuming that your judgment is correct, this immediately yields a possible way out of a negative emotion, namely, by revising the evaluation. After all, sometimes events that initially seem bad turn out in the long run to have important positive consequences that outweigh the initial suffering.

In any case, please accept that fact that nobody except you is making either the initial judgment or the egocentric evaluation. Negative emotions certainly don't feel good. The truth is that, whenever you are in the grip of one, you have done that to yourself.

So, accept full responsibility for the quality of your own emotional life.

Second, **avoid trying to ignore negative emotions.** This only postpones the inevitable and often makes suffering worse.

A negative emotion won't disappear just because you distract yourself from attending to it. It will still be there leaking poison into your life. Ignoring a negative passion can be as foolish as ignoring a diagnosis of cancer.

When you have a big problem, admit it. You may or may not be able to solve it, but big problems almost never get solved accidentally or by magic. Dealing effectively with a major problem requires admitting that the problem is real.

Besides, why lie to yourself? That's all you are doing if you pretend not to notice a problem. In order to pretend that it isn't real, you must think of its reality. "The emotion I'm feeling right now isn't real" is a very odd judgment.

Emotions are natural and, so, not feeling emotions would be unnatural. Notice when you are feeling emotions. If a loved one dies and you feel sad, your sadness won't disappear just because you are trying to ignore it since it's unpleasant. In fact, as I argue in what follows, this is exactly the opposite of what you should do.

Third, **avoid venting.** Venting is acting on the basis of a negative passion. For example, you get fired from your job and then punch a wall or get into a fist fight.

As a cure for negative passions, venting fails because it violates a fundamental psychological law, namely, whatever we think about expands in importance. The more you vent, the more you are thinking about your negative emotion; the more you are thinking about your negative emotion, the more important it becomes. Because it makes the emotion more powerful, venting only perpetuates or even increases your emotional distress, your emotional suffering.

Since right actions diminish pain or suffering while wrong actions perpetuate or increase pain or suffering and since venting perpetuates or increases pain or suffering, venting is wrong. In fact, it's a paradigmatic example of a wrong action.

Distinguish physical pain from suffering. Physical pain goes with being alive. If you experience pain from a broken bone or tooth ache, for example, that's just a symptom of being alive. That's not the same as suffering (dissatisfaction, discontent, unease, sorrow, misery, sadness, <u>dukkha</u>), which is optional. Pain occasionally happens, but suffering is what we (usually unintentionally) do to ourselves.

Suffering usually prompts one of two extreme responses. First, "Oh, woe is me! Why do these things always happen to me? I was born to suffer." Obviously, that response will just keep you stuck. Second, "What is life trying to teach me by giving me this distress? How can I turn this suffering around and live better?" That response prompts a search for a better alternative.

An important negative emotion can seem like a huge obstacle to living better, but it is always also an opportunity for learning better how to live well. Your response to it is solely your responsibility. If you will seize the opportunity and use it to teach yourself how to do better emotionally, **there is no reason that, from an emotional perspective, your life cannot keep getting better and better.** That's really good news.

Before turning negative emotions around, at least avoid making them worse by either trying to ignore them or venting them. The wisdom of the middle way begins with *taking time out.* Be still and focus on the emotion. It may well be uncomfortable to do so, but, before too long, the discomfort will ease.

I like to think of it this way: all thoughts insist on their own importance. Whenever they arise, they want attention. They hate it when they are ignored. If you will learn to pay full attention to them even briefly, that will please them and they'll bother you less. Notice them fully, let them go, and get back to doing whatever you should be doing.

Don't fight them. Instead, accept them. In fact, welcome them! They are important experiences. Befriend them. Pay attention to them. Love them to death.

In terms of improving the quality of your emotional life (living well emotionally, flourishing emotionally), that's the only way that works well. Let's examine exactly how to do that.

7: How to Dissolve Negative Emotions

Negative emotions are normal. There's nothing wrong with you if you sometimes find yourself overwhelmed by anger, fear, sadness, loneliness, or other powerful passions.

What's not normal is being able to dissolve them skillfully. If you learn how to do that, you'll have learned one of the most important skills required for living well (mastering life, being wise). That learning requires understanding and practice. You are gaining the understanding reading this book, but the practicing will be up to you.

Suppose that one of the many powerful negative emotions is troubling you. What should you do? I recommend that you follow these 7 steps for dealing with negative emotions.

First, **accept full responsibility for your situation.** *No event or other person is able to affect you emotionally without your consent.* It's impossible. Even though it was not intentional, you have put yourself in this position. Your emotions wouldn't exist except for your thoughts and your bodily reactions to those thoughts.

The *good news* is that, since you got yourself into it, you have the potential to get yourself out of it.

We weren't given instruction manuals at birth informing us how to live well emotionally. It's something that we must learn how to do. Since you are learning how to do it by reading this book, good for you.

Second, **identify the most troubling emotion.**

You may have the false belief that it is easy to identify what you are feeling. "Alexithymics" are people who don't know what they are feeling. They find having a negative emotion not only baffling but overwhelming. It is certainly not self-evident to them what they are feeling.

Alexithymics often "somaticize," which is thinking that emotional distress is just bodily distress. So they may pursue medical diagnosis and treatment instead of what they really need, which is emotional treatment.

Furthermore, even though it is unlikely that you suffer from alexithymia, it can still be difficult to identify what you are feeling. The reason for that is that, frequently, two emotions can become linked. For example, fear often precedes and follows anger. In fact, powerful emotions only infrequently occur one at a time. Passions can alternate in a rapid sequence, and they can even blend together. Furthermore, one can stimulate another as when you become angry at yourself for, say, becoming afraid.

It takes deliberate effort and practice to know yourself well emotionally.

Third, **identify what triggered that emotion.**

This, too, is not always easy to do. Emotional responses that you learned during your life become involuntary. They can be so automatic that they are very difficult to notice. (This is why the next step is important.)

You should now understand that emotions don't just happen. They are not irrational events like that just wash over us like weather fronts. We do emotions to ourselves. When we untangle them and analyze them, we discover that *emotions are intelligible reactions of the egoic mind to protect us.*

Something always causes the "This is bad for me" judgment at the heart of every negative emotion. What is it?

Fourth, **keep a written log about the negative emotions that are most troubling you.**

This is a way of determining exactly what your emotional habits are. It's similar to keeping a food diary: if you are not aware of what you are regularly putting into your mouth, how could you improve your nutritional program? Keeping a log is a way of getting to understand yourself better. It increases awareness.

With respect to the most troublesome one, what, exactly, was the judgment that you made? What triggered it? Which evaluation did you make? Exactly how did you feel as a result? What exactly are you saying to yourself about it right now?

Fifth, **question the initial judgment and the evaluation.**

Occasionally, the initial judgments are incorrect. If so and you internalize that, the subsequent emotion will fade away.

The egocentric evaluations are always dubious. Why?

The fact is that, like the rest of us, you don't know the future. Since the future is unknown and unknowable, the future consequences of the event that triggered your response are unknown and unknowable. In the long run, your initial evaluation could prove wrong.

How many times in the past has something happened that, although you thought at the time was good, turned out later to have very bad consequences? How many times in the past has something happened that, although you thought at the time was bad, turned out later to have very good consequences?

So, although the physiological sensations that depend upon the egocentric evaluation may be unpleasant or uncomfortable, their very existence is actually precarious. Even when they are unpleasant or uncomfortable, experiencing them cannot hurt you; in fact, trying not to experience them can lead to a lot more damage than just letting them be and fully experiencing them. If you really do learn from them, that may change the egocentric evaluation from "bad" to "good," which may enable you simply to let them go.

Questioning your evaluation in this way automatically weakens it. By accepting the emotion, you are identifying it as part of your life. The emotion is a peculiar kind of motivational or energy form and, simply by examining it, you are treating it the same way it's possible to examine all forms. No forms have a sacred standing. All are questionable. All are denizens of Becoming. In the sense that they all have that same standing or status, they are all equal and they are all temporary.

Sixth, and critically, **use some body practice or other to release the emotion.**

Body practices are nothing but trainings that pay attention to your body. There's nothing whatsoever mysterious, esoteric, religious, or magical about them.

Your body is part of you. It's a part of you that you typically take for granted because you are paying attention to thoughts that lead you elsewhere. Body practices simply bring you home to the body.

Body practices are the classic way to realize what we actually are, in other words, to become a sage. It's impossible to tell simply by looking at someone whether he or she is or isn't a sage. Sages are really distinguished by *how* they do what they do rather than usually by *what* they do. Since it's possible only to observe what it done (and not always how it is done), it's usually impossible to tell from observation who is a sage and who isn't.

Perhaps you have known many sages. Perhaps you have known none. Even if you lack role models, it's possible to learn how to emulate what sages do for yourself. There are many ways to emulate them, and I explain one simple, easy way in the next chapter.

Please realize that, since all sages live well emotionally, **living well emotionally is possible**. Furthermore, since there's no essential difference between you and me and sages, living well emotionally is as possible for you and me as it is for sages. That's really good news!

Sages master the middle way of dealing with emotions. They avoid the two counter-productive extremes of venting and ignoring. Instead, they take a time out and let emotions be. Nothing else is needed to live well emotionally.

As always, complete nonresistance to reality, fully accepting what-is exactly as it is, is the key to peacefulness and tranquility. Sages are characterized by such nonresistance, whereas fools are characterized by resistance. This explains the foolishness of negativity, which is just another form of resistance.

Probably, you even may have some relevant experience of this yourself. Perhaps, for example, when you were a child you got into a fight with a sibling and your mother made you stand in the corner for ten minutes. Why?

She did not want you to vent, to act on the basis of your anger or whatever other negative emotions were fueling your behavior. On the other hand, she didn't want you to ignore what had just been happening. She wanted you to focus, without distraction, on your life for ten minutes.

Sages master the art of taking times out. It's that simple. Why not emulate them? I explain one way to do that in the next chapter.

8: Body Practice

There are different kinds of body practices. There is no one that works best for everyone; in particular, there is no one that works best for promoting emotional well-being.

If you already have a body practice that is working for you, just do it more intensely if it is not yet producing the degree of emotional well-being you'd like. If that ultimately fails, either replace it with a different body practice or supplement it with a different body practice.

The easiest body practice to master is what let's call "aliveness awareness." (There's no standard terminology.)

Your body is alive. You already understand that, but do you actually feel it? Probably not – because it's quite likely that you are almost always lost in thought. Focusing on (paying attention to, becoming aware of) the aliveness that is always available in your own body is one excellent way to break free from compulsive thoughts. It's a way of shifting from thinking to awareness.

It's not a substitute for experiencing emotions bodily. Again, whenever you are suffering from a powerful negative emotion, give yourself the gift of a time out and simply focus on what that emotion feels like as a set of bodily sensations. Still yourself physically and then focus on them. Do not judge or evaluate them; just accept them even when they are uncomfortable, even when they hurt. It's alright: they crave acceptance. They are part of your life and, if you resist them, you are just creating separation and, so, suffering. Doing that will worsen the situation rather than make it better. Just notice them and focus on them for a while until their power wanes and they disappear.

The stronger they are, the longer you'll need to focus on them. Just do whatever it takes. 'Do' here does not mean acting or behaving; it simply refers to paying attention for as long as necessary. If you need to sit quietly several times before those bodily sensations that are parts of the emotion fade, then sit quietly several times. If you need to cry, then cry.

It's true that the last thing you may want to do is to face what you are feeling. Yet that is what sages do and the only alternative is to try to distract yourself unto death. It's your choice. Why not emulate the wise?

Standing up to that powerful emotion can seem draining. Here's how to restore your energy naturally.

Aliveness awareness is based on the fact that it is possible to **experience your life energy directly.** Again, normally you are so lost in thought that you are separated from your body. Again, separation is always the root cause of suffering. So, by being separated from your body, you are, unintentionally, causing yourself to suffer.

Body practices go back at least to the Axial Age 2500 years ago. They have been promoted by the wise since before the time of The Buddha and are promoted today by such excellent teachers as Eckhart Tolle and Thich Nhat Hanh.

Not only isn't there anything original about this presentation of aliveness awareness, it would be very strange if there were. Despite our natural bias in favor of our contemporaries, they are neither the only nor the original font of wisdom.

Body practices involve focusing on the "inner" body, in other words, on physiological sensations that seem to arise inside the body. They ignore what is external to the body. They have nothing to do with the appearance or shape of the body.

Bodies, physical objects, are ultimately shimmering clumps of energy. In that sense, the world is alive. If you think that the world is dead, that's only because you are stuck in the egoic mind using concepts, which deaden life. Anyone who has ever cared for a house or an automobile realizes that they deteriorate as time goes by; they never stay the same. You know from your own living body that it is aging; sometimes we are very aware that our bodies are in incessant flux.

It turns out that it's extremely useful to let go of thinking about our bodies; it's extremely useful to bypass our intellects and directly experience them. Drop all worries about conceptualizing and understanding.

Why? After all, don't we want to let go of experiencing ourselves physically in order to awaken?

No. It's counter-intuitive, but that kind of thinking is exactly backwards.

By practicing aliveness awareness you are actually freeing yourself from identification with the body. Yes, you are your body, but you are much more than your body. To get stuck *only* identifying with your body eliminates the possibility of identifying with more than your body. So it's good to free yourself from identification with it.

How, though, could aliveness awareness work? After all, it would seem that by paying greater attention to physiological sensations we are strengthening identification with the body rather than weakening it. Because the body is subject to illness, aging, and death, it generates fear.

The truth is that we are our bodies. Also, however, the truth is that we are more than our bodies.

Please do not confuse the physical body with its aliveness. *It's by establishing and maintaining a connection with its aliveness that we become anchored in the present.* This is critical, because life only occurs in the present; it cannot occur yesterday or tomorrow.

The more you focus attention on aliveness, the less attention there is for "thoughting" or compulsive thinking. It's thoughting that obscures the insight that we are more than our bodies, that we are, to use my preferred terminology, not only temporal Becoming but also eternal Being.

The reason aliveness awareness works is the same reason that all body practices work: it works by freeing us from compulsive thoughts. All body practices provide a physical locus for awareness. For example, that locus for meditation is breathing. If you focus on that locus, you are practicing properly; if you focus on anything else, you are not practicing properly. In fact, you may only be thinking instead of practicing.

Normally the mind focuses on whatever it wants. This is its untrained (undisciplined, unpurified) state. Attention jumps around madly like a troop of monkeys moving through the forest canopy.

When you initially try to train (discipline, purify) it, it resists just as a wild horse resists when you initially try to ride it. Taming the mind is like taming a wild horse: it requires effort and patience. Humor helps. The mind, like the horse, becomes much more useful when tamed.

The point of taming the mind, the point of practicing or training, is to diminish the power of compulsive thoughting and open to the power of awareness, which is awake consciousness without conceptualizing. This is sometimes called "no-mind" or "no-thought." It comes from moment-to-moment awareness. Focusing on aliveness is one of the best ways, and probably the easiest way, to open to this creative state.

You are not always experiencing emotions, which is why the physiological sensations that are parts of emotions are not good locus points for attention when training the mind. By way of contrast, the aliveness of the body is always there and, so, always available for training the mind.

Although I'm not sure about this, it's also possible that, by training the mind using aliveness awareness, we are actually benefitting the body by strengthening its ability to heal itself.

Nonjudgmental noticing of aliveness is accepting life just as it is. It's practicing nonresistance. It opens us to the source of ease and lightness; it opens us to the source of grace. It frees us from incessantly focusing on forms in Becoming by revealing formless Being.

Here's **how to do aliveness awareness**.

Begin by putting your body in a comfortable position resting on your back. You may use a recliner or not.

Using a recliner is ideal for me. Sit on the recliner and push it completely back. Keep your legs together and completely relaxed; do not cross them. Rest your hands on your hips or on the arms of the recliner, whichever is more comfortable. Keep your upper arms next to your torso. Relax your arms, shoulders and neck.

If you lack access to a recliner or prefer not to use one, simply lie on your back. Put a pillow or two under your knees to reduce the tension on your lower back. You may put a small pillow under your head if you want. Keep your legs together and completely relaxed; do not cross them. Rest your hands on your hips or next to your body, whichever is more comfortable. Keep your upper arms next to your torso. Relax your arms, shoulders and neck.

Initially, it may help to close your eyes. On the other hand, of course, if you are tired or sleepy, closing them may just encourage sleep.

Once you are in position, be still. If, for example, your nose itches, do not scratch it. Keep still (and the temptation to itch will soon disappear anyway).

Focus on feeling the insides of your hands. That's it. Just stay focused on whatever is going on inside your hands. There is life energy there and it's only a matter of a little time and patience to experience it directly if you don't experience it immediately.

Don't worry! Your hands are alive and the energy is there. If you don't feel anything in 10 or 15 minutes, that's not a problem (unless you make it one). Just repeat the practice tomorrow and the day after that and the day after that and so on until you begin to feel it. It may take a week or two, but so what?

Once you awaken to the aliveness, you may just feel something subtle and peculiar in a knuckle or one finger of one hand. That's it! You are alive and you are, perhaps for the first time, feeling alive. Keep focusing on it.

Soon, perhaps the next day, you'll feel it in a whole finger and in a whole hand. Then put your attention inside the other hand. Soon, you'll feel it there as well.

Once you are feeling it inside both hands, pay attention to what your feet feel like from the inside. Of course, your feet are relaxed. It's often easier to feel the aliveness inside your feet than inside your hands. Soon, you'll be able to feel it inside both feet and both hands.

Then focus on feeling it up the front of your legs from your shins to your thighs. Similarly, focus on feeling it in your forearms and then in your upper arms. Eventually, you'll be able to feel it in your shoulders and right into your torso.

Aliveness is a peculiar feeling. Initially, it may feel rather like a very mild tingling. Once you get good at it, you'll be able to lie still for 30 or 60 minutes and it feels really good -- somewhat like there's a tingling or very mild electric current running through you. I sometimes wonder why my arms and legs don't levitate on their own accord. (As usual, language doesn't work well in such matters.)

Practice this every day for a while – at least until you really are getting a strong feeling of aliveness. Work up to feeling it for half an hour or an hour without distraction.

Soon you will not even have to close your eyes to do it. There'll be no problem looking around.

As you get better and better at it, it will increase in intensity, which may wash up and down your body in waves.

Furthermore, within a few weeks you'll be able to do it sitting up as long as you are still. Eventually, you'll be able to do it when you are not even still.

If, as I do, you relax sometimes watching television, please do it while you watch television. Why not? Ideally, extend it throughout all your activities.

The point is to make doing aliveness awareness a habit. This is a nurturing practice that fosters the transition from incessant "thoughting" to awareness. The more you practice, the more you'll be rewarded.

What you are actually practicing is freedom from compulsive thoughts. What you are actually doing is diminishing the power of thoughts. Eventually, the idea is always to be grounded in aliveness and never again to be lost in a storm of thoughts.

It not only feels good, but it's one of the classic ways to train the mind. There are other kinds of practices. Some involve doing "inner body" scans. The various forms of meditation involve focusing on the physical process of breathing. Some involve using the body for prostrations. And so on.

If you'd rather do a different kind of body practice, that's fine. What's important is to do some kind of body practice daily that is effective for you.

The more you practice properly, the more you are training the mind. The more you train the mind, the more you will free yourself from emotional bondage.

This is particularly true in the case of negative emotions. I don't know what image comes to mind when you think of a sage, but it is surely not of someone who is emotionally distraught. It will be someone who enjoys peace of mind, if not perpetually at least frequently.

The way to foster living well emotionally is the same as the way to foster any kind of peace of mind, namely, by using a body practice to train the mind, which frees it from compulsive thoughts. Perhaps 80 or 90% of thoughts are repetitive, stale, useless, boring, and obstructive. These are the compulsive ones that we are better off without. They seem endlessly to circle around like clothes in a dryer.

All classic body practices work to free us from this endless circling. They leave us free to focus, when necessary, only on thinking that is fresh, creative, original, and useful.

The mind becomes more efficient when so trained; it becomes better at thinking when it is freed from addiction to compulsive thoughts. Its ability to focus is strengthened.

So please make aliveness awareness or some other body practice a daily habit. The more you practice properly, the more it will benefit you. It's not only a way of feeling more alive in the present moment, it's a way of getting beyond the prison of conceptual thinking.

Everyone is able to do this. **There's no scarcity of peace of mind.** Since there's an abundance, please help yourself to as much as you want.

It opens us to our True Nature, which is nothing less than Being. Again, since thinking requires concepts and all concepts are principles of separation (classification, division, sorting, dividing), thinking cannot grasp unity, which is the absence of separation. This is why it is impossible to think Being. Being is unity.

Because emotions require separation, which is indicated by the "for me" that is at the heart of every emotion, emotions also block awareness of Being. In other words, all thoughts and emotions are nothing more than forms, denizens of Becoming. Incessantly focusing on them obstructs awareness of Being.

Why is this so harmful?

It's because we are human beings. To be human is to be a form (actually, a set of forms) in Becoming, but we are also formless Being. Remaining trapped in Becoming blocks awareness of our true nature.

In other words, it's as if we had one foot in temporal Becoming and the other foot in non-temporal Being. Human beings are both forms and what is formless. Human life focused solely on forms in Becoming cannot be, therefore, balanced or centered. It is only sages who enjoy balanced lives that are peaceful.

Since Being is formless, it is either apprehended *non*conceptually or not at all. This is why it's critical to drop all thoughts and open to the direct apprehension of Being. Dropping all thoughts, which is the purpose of all body practices, includes dropping all egocentric evaluations such as those at the heart of every emotion.

This is **the only way to abiding joy**. As long as you remain stuck riding the emotional roller coaster up and down, you'll never experience *abiding* joy. The only joy experienced will be limited in duration as well as dependent on fleeting forms.

Awakening from the prison of forms is liberation or freedom from the temporal. It requires the end of all thinking, which is the stopping or complete stilling of the mind. It's impossible to think and simultaneously be aware of the eternal (Being). Just pay full attention to nothing (no thing, no form, emptiness).

You are normal if you are unbalanced. Sadly, it is still the case that sages that are few and far between. There is no necessity, however, that that remains the case. There is no reason why we need to continue to think of ourselves as slaves to time, which all sages assure us is the greatest obstacle to awakening.

There is nothing you need to do or gain. Why? You already are what you are. Realizing what you are doesn't take any time. As my teacher once said, just select all thoughts and delete.

Doing that, opening to Oneness, will not only free you from the fear with which most humans live, but also it will flood your life is love and grace. Why? Because there is no time in Being, there are also no problems or any dissatisfaction in Being.

This is important because the ego/I needs problems. The more enemies it has, the stronger it feels. Without enemies, without problems, it weakens and dies. It is this ego attrition that is the wonderful outcome of mastering a body practice. The result is a state of loving openness to all beings, which is the beginning of authentic love and the end of egoic self-delusion.

Furthermore, your opening fully to the present moment will help others as well as yourself. The better you live, the more you will be indirectly helping others to live better. [If these topics interest you, I suggest my Getting Things Done and Love and Respect as well as Tolle's The Power of Now.]

Therefore, dealing the right way with emotional eating can lead to wisdom (living well, abiding joy). Emotional eating seems like a curse, but it's actually a disguised opportunity for improving the quality of your life.

Best wishes!

Selected Bibliography

Abram, David. The Spell of the Sensuous.

Bayda, Ezra. Beyond Happiness.

Beck, Charlotte Joko. Everyday Zen.

Beck, Charlotte Joko. Nothing Special.

Begley, Sharon. Train Your Mind Change Your Brain.

Bradford, Dennis. "Beyond Skepticism in Ethics" in The Philosophy of Panayot Butchavrov (Larry Lee Blackman, ed.).

Bradford, Dennis. Compulsive Overeating Help.

Bradford, Dennis. How to Eat Less – Easily!

Bradford, Dennis. How to Stop Emotional Eating.

Bradford, Dennis. Mastery in 7 Steps.

Bradford, Dennis. The Fundamental Ideas.

Bradford, Dennis. The Meditative Approach to Philosophy.

Bradford, Dennis. The Three Things the Rest of Us Should Know about Zen Training.

Bradford, D., & Wright, A. Belly Fat Blast.

Buddha, The. Basic Teachings of the Buddha. (Glenn Wallis, ed.)

Buddha, The. In the Buddha's Words (Bhikkhu Bodhi, ed.).

Butchvarov, Panayot. Being Qua Being.

Butchvarov, Panayot. Skepticism About the External World.

Butchvarov, Panayot. Skepticism in Ethics.

Butchvarov, Panayot. The Concept of Knowledge.

Dalai Lama, The, & Cutler, Howard. The Art of Happiness.

Eckman, Paul. Emotions Revealed (revised edition).

Emerson, R. W. Essays of Ralph Waldo Emerson.

Gilbert, Daniel. Stumbling on Happiness.

Goleman, Daniel. Emotional Intelligence.

Goleman, Daniel. Vital Lies, Simple Truths.

Kapleau, Philip. The Three Pillars of Zen (25th anniversary edition).

Kornfield, Jack. A Path With Heart.

Lao-Tzu. TAOTECHING (Red Pine, tr.)

Norretranders, Tor. The User Illusion. (Jonathan Sydenham, tr.)

Sartre, Jean-Paul. Being and Nothingness. (Hazel E. Barnes, tr.)

Sartre, Jean-Paul. The Psychology of Imagination.

Sartre, Jean-Paul. The Transcendence of the Ego.

Solomon, Robert C. The Passions.

Suzuki, Shunryu. Zen Mind, Beginner's Mind.

Taylor, Jill Bolte. <u>My Stroke of Insight</u>.

Tolle, Eckhart. <u>A New Earth.</u>

Tolle, Eckhart. "Creating A New Earth"

Tolle, Eckhart. "Even the Sun Will Die."

Tolle, Eckhart. "Finding Your Life's Purpose."

Tolle, Eckhart. "Living the Liberated Life and Dealing with the Pain-Body."

Tolle, Eckhart. "Realizing the Power of Now."

Tolle, Eckhart. <u>The Power of Now.</u>

Tolle, Eckhart. "The Realization of Being."

Tolle, Eckhart. "Through the Open Door."

About the Author

I was born 3 July 1946 in Teaneck, New Jersey, U.S.A. I graduated with a diploma from Blair Academy in 1964. I was a pre-professional philosophy major at Syracuse University and graduated in 1968. After two years as an Army lieutenant with overseas duty in Korea from 1969-1971, I attended graduate school at The University of Iowa where I received an M.A. (1974) and a Ph.D. (1977).

I taught humanities and philosophy at SUNY Geneseo from 1977 to 2009. I've authored over twenty books. I founded the Ironox Works, Inc., publishing company in 2004. [http://ironoxworks.com]

I'm a former member of MENSA and the American Philosophical Association. I played hockey for many years in the Rochester Metro Hockey League. I've been a member of the Rochester Zen Center for about twenty years. I live peacefully and happily in solitude in a cottage on the shore the westernmost of the Finger Lakes in upstate New York.

For more, please visit my Amazon Author Central page:

http://www.amazon.com/-/e/B0047EI11A

Social media contact information: http://www.twitter.com/dennisebradford http://www.facebook.com/dennis.bradford.313 http://www.linkedin.com/pub/dennis-e-bradford/1a/a2a/5214/

I encourage you to visit my blog on wisdom and well-being: http://dennis-bradford.com. Its posts are grouped in terms of six kinds of well-being (in no particular order) on the sidebar, namely, financial, moral (inter-personal), intellectual, physical, emotional, and spiritual. I encourage you to begin with whatever interests you most. Please feel free to leave comments. I happen to think that there's an enormous amount of valuable, free content there.

If you are interested in finding out more about my other books, they are available at: http://www.amazon.com. Simply select 'Books' or 'Kindle Store' and do a search for 'Dennis E Bradford'.

Thank you for reading this book.

I've a **favor** to ask: would you please leave some feedback about this book? Whether it benefits me or not, others would surely benefit from your judgment. Simply go to Books at Amazon.com, type in 'emotional eating bradford,' and scroll down the page that opens to leave a comment. Thank you in advance.

For More Help

Tolle's THE POWER OF NOW

Bradford's HOW TO STOP EMOTIONAL EATING

Bradford's MASTERY IN 7 STEPS

www.ingramcontent.com/pod-product-compliance
Lightning Source LLC
Chambersburg PA
CBHW062114040426
42337CB00042B/2391